This Book
Belongs
to

.....Clint Justice.....
♥ 90

♥ For Lily ♥

First American edition, 1988.
Text and illustrations copyright © 1988 by Sophie Windham
All rights reserved. Published simultaneously in Canada.
Created and produced by Sadie Fields Productions Ltd., London.
Printed and bound in Italy.
Library of Congress Cataloging-in-Publication Data
Windham, Sophie. Noah's Ark.
(A peek-through-the-window book)
Summary: Retells the story of how Noah and the animals
survived the flood. Features peek-through-the-window illustrations.
1. Noah (Biblical figure) – Juvenile literature.
2. Noah's ark – Juvenile literature. 3. Deluge –
Juvenile literature. 4. Bible. O.T. – Biography –
Juvenile literature. 5. Toy and movable books – Specimens.
(1. Noah's ark. 2. Bible stories – O.T.
3. Toy and movable books) 1. Title.
BS580.N6W56 1988 222'.1109505 88-5935
ISBN 0-399-21564-6
G.P. Putnam's Sons, 200 Madison Avenue, New York, NY 10016
First impression.

NOAH'S ARK

A Peek-Through-the-Window Book

by Sophie Windham

G.P. Putnam's Sons   New York

Noah had been behaving strangely.

Sometimes he'd look up and nod.

Sometimes he'd look down and frown.

And all the time he seemed to be talking to himself.

But Mrs. Noah said nothing until one evening   .   .   .

…when he came running into the house shouting,

"It's going to rain. We've got to build a boat!"

"Wouldn't an umbrella do?" asked Mrs. Noah.

"Not a thousand umbrellas! And not a moment to lose!

It's going to rain. And rain. And rain!"

Outside the wind blew and blew and blew.

Inside Noah drew and drew and drew.

When he had finished,

Mrs. Noah brought them tea, and

Noah showed her his plans.

"There's going to be a mighty flood," puffed Noah.

"The rains will begin next Thursday. Even the tops of the highest

mountains are going to be covered by the sea!"

"People have not taken care of the world

and we've been chosen to save the animals.

I've been gathering branches to build an ark."

The next day Noah finished sawing wood

and the day after that he started building his ark.

At last it was finished and Noah said to Mrs. Noah,

"Now we must gather up all the animals in the world."

There were so many animals to find.

Stripey ones and spotty ones and muddy ones.

They chose two of every kind.

A male and female of each.

Shiny ones and hairy ones and bald ones.

And two by two they came to Noah's ark,

which was finished just in time.

Mrs. Noah had stocked the ark wit

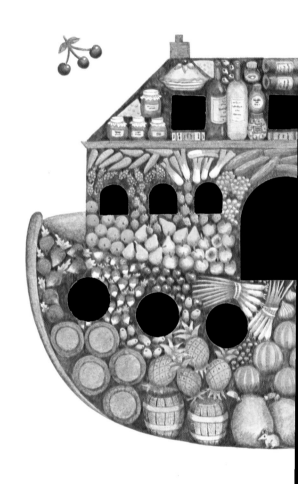

And she obviously had tho

. . . because there was food for every kind of animal.

At last all of the animals were snug and cosy inside.

Then, with not a moment to spare

the sun said "Goodbye."

And the windows of heaven opened

and rain poured down.

And soon,

puddles formed pools.

Pools became lakes.

And lakes became seas.

And when the seas joined together, the ark

floated up on dark and angry waters covering the land.

For forty days and forty nights it rained.

Storms followed gales, and gales followed storms.

Until finally, after the worst storm of all,

the last little raindrop went "*plop*."

, a strange face peered over the edge of the world,

eautiful light woke Noah and his wife.

It was the sun! The wonderful yellow sun! They dresse

A rainbow soared across the sky. But for as far as the t

there was nothing but water. So Noah sent a

and in the evening, she returned with a tiny new

"We are saved!" cried Noah. "The land is saved."

"The animals are saved! And the trees and flowers.

The world is saved!"

"Hooray!" said all the creatures in the ark.

"I never realized how beautiful even a little daisy is,"

Noah said, "– not until they all disappeared."

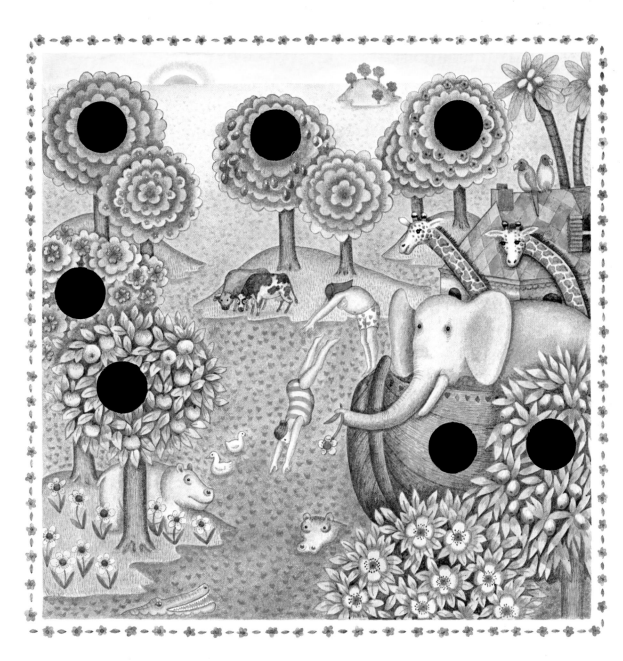

"We must never risk losing the world again," said Mrs. Noah.

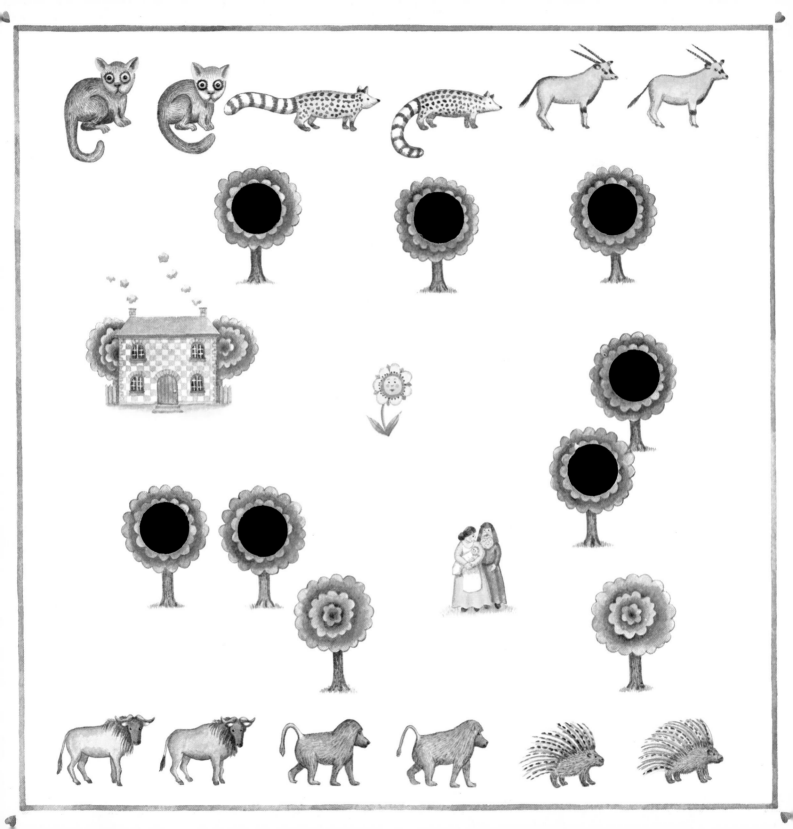